LIGHT

BY STEWART ROSS

TULIP BOOKS®

Text by Stewart Ross in cooperation with Christine Clover.
© copyright in this edition Tulip Books 2019

ISBN 978-1-78388-148-2

Index

Always there

People did not really *discover* light. Like fire, it was on the Earth from the beginning.

What we *have* discovered is what light is, and how to make it for ourselves.

WOW!

The Sun is our biggest source of light: it is 400,000 times brighter than a full moon!

Early ideas

The ancient Greek scientist Euclid was one of the first people to think seriously about light.

» He said we see because rays come out of our eyes onto the objects before us.

I NEVER KNEW!

Euclid said near objects are sharper than distant ones because more of our 'visual rays' fall on them!

7

Lenses

Back in ancient times, people noticed how objects looked different when seen through a **lens**.

Early lenses were made of a natural **mineral**, like **quartz**.

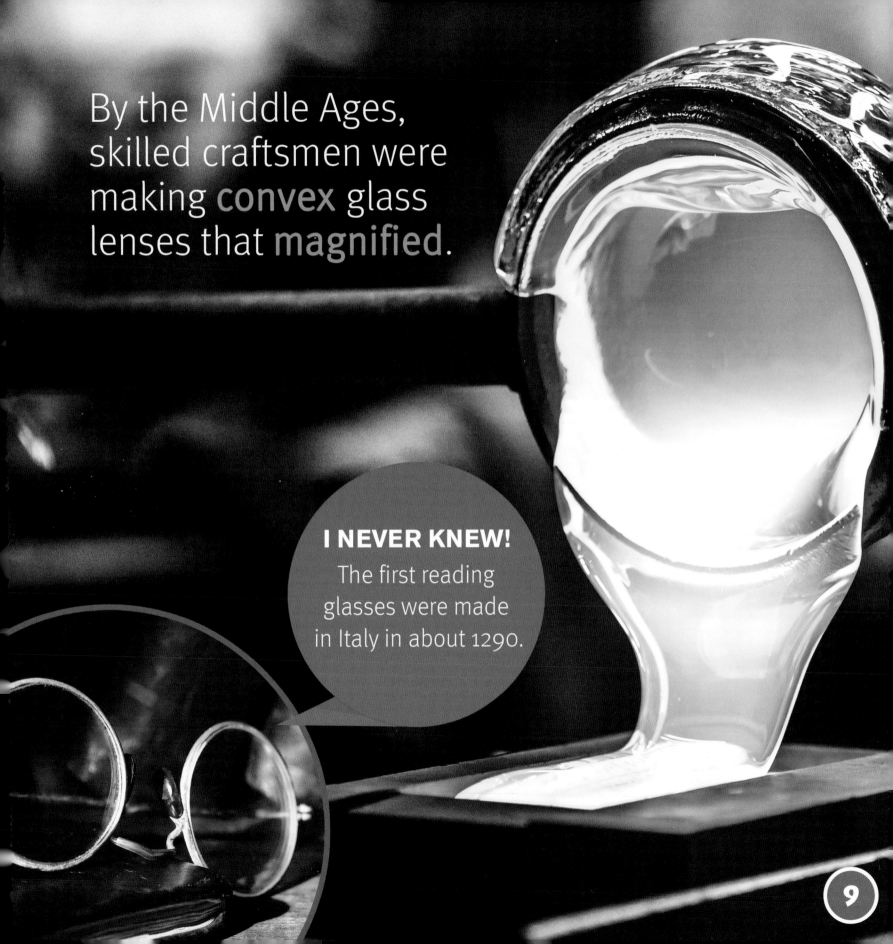

By the Middle Ages, skilled craftsmen were making **convex** glass lenses that **magnified**.

I NEVER KNEW!
The first reading glasses were made in Italy in about 1290.

The telescope

The first **telescopes** were made in the 17th century. There were two types.

I NEVER KNEW!

When the Italian scientist Galileo looked at the moon through his home-made telescope, he saw not a shining disc but mountains and craters!

Refracting telescopes used glass lenses to collect light from distant objects.

Reflecting telescopes gathered light with mirrors.

The spectrum

Scientists knew how light behaved,
but they still did not know what it was.

Sir Isaac Newton (1643–1727) suggested it was 'coloured **particles**'.

Using a prism, he showed white light was a **spectrum** of colours.

I NEVER KNEW!

In 1690, the Dutch scientist Christiaan Huygens argued that light is a wave – and he was right!

Waves and photons

In the 19th century, scientists realised light waves were **magnetic**.
The magnetism came from electricity.

In the 20th century, Albert Einstein discovered that light was made up of the tiniest particles, called **photons**.

Light in nature

Light is essential for life on Earth. Plants **react** to light in three ways:

- *Photosynthesis* – using the light energy from the sun.

- *Phototropism* – moving towards light.

- *Photoperiodism* – behaving according to how light or dark it is.

I NEVER KNEW!
The face of a sunflower follows the Sun, moving east to west during the day!

Making light

For thousands of years, we lit our homes with candles and oil lamps.

In 1792, gas lighting was invented.

In the next century, electric lights took over. As a result, our homes and cities shine like beacons!

I NEVER KNEW!
The first light bulb lasted just 40 hours!

Lasers and night vision

In 1960, a new type of light appeared: the laser. Lasers **focus** light energy very sharply to produce strong, bright beams.

Scientists have also invented goggles that allow us to see in the dark.

I NEVER KNEW!

Snakes detect **infrared** light, which we cannot see, by using special **sensors** on their heads!

21

Light pollution

Too much light pollutes the environment. Plants, animals and people become confused if it never gets dark.

Doctors say that we need darkness to sleep properly – light pollution can make us ill.

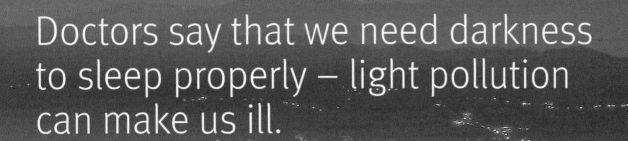

I NEVER KNEW!

Astronomers hate light pollution because it stops them observing the stars and planets clearly.

Glossary

Infrared
Light at the end of the spectrum beyond the colour red.

Lens
A shaped piece of glass for directing light.

Magnify
Make something appear larger than it is.

Mineral
A natural substance found in the ground.

Quartz
A hard, clear mineral.

Magnetic
Able to attract metal.

Particle
A very, very small piece of something.

Photon
A strange, minute particle that creates light.

React
To respond.

Reflection
When light comes back off a surface.

Refraction
When light changes direction as it passes from one substance to another.

Sensor
A device that feels movement, temperature, etc.

Spectrum
The spread of light we can see; it is best seen in a rainbow.

Telescope
A device for looking closely at distant objects.